T0316853

THE FRAMEWORK
of an
ORDERED SOCIETY

THE FRAMEWORK
OF AN
ORDERED SOCIETY

———————

By
SIR ARTHUR SALTER
K.C.B.

———————

CAMBRIDGE
AT THE UNIVERSITY PRESS
1933

CAMBRIDGE
UNIVERSITY PRESS

University Printing House, Cambridge CB2 8BS, United Kingdom

Cambridge University Press is part of the University of Cambridge.

It furthers the University's mission by disseminating knowledge in the pursuit of education, learning and research at the highest international levels of excellence.

www.cambridge.org
Information on this title: www.cambridge.org/9781107453593

First published 1933
First paperback edition 2014

A catalogue record for this publication is available from the British Library

ISBN 978-1-107-45359-3 Paperback

CONTENTS

PREFATORY NOTE

A LECTURESHIP has recently been established in memory of Alfred Marshall, the duties of the lecturer being to give in the year of office three lectures, or such other number as the Faculty Board of Economics and Politics may approve, dealing with "some development of Economics or of Economic History or of some kindred subject".

Sir Arthur Salter was appointed as the first Alfred Marshall Lecturer, and delivered the three lectures which are here reprinted at Cambridge on February 22, 23 and 24, 1933.

These lectures do not attempt to present a novel contribution to either economic thought or practical policy. A good deal of work has been done in the last few years both by individuals and by societies in developing the idea of a planned society. In some of this work the lecturer has been privileged to participate. His conception of a new society is therefore partly derived from others, partly individual. He has presented it in relation to his general economic thought in *Recovery: The Second Effort*. He here discusses some of the principles on which it is based in a form designed to stimulate thought and enquiry among his audience of members of Cambridge University. He has tried to sketch, in bare and tentative outline, a ground plan which he hopes may encourage others to build.

I

THE NEED FOR A NEW SYSTEM

I is now nine years since Alfred Marshall died, and nine decades since he was born. It would be presumption for one who is a member neither of his University nor of his profession to attempt to add more than the most modest of laurels to his wreath. His place is established securely as the first of modern economists, continuing as he did the great tradition of the English economists and bequeathing it to his successors, especially to those of his own University which maintains in his science the leadership which he established.

Two characteristics, however, of his work and life I may venture to recall. First, he was a better economist for being more than an economist. His range of interest, extending over ethics and metaphysics, and philosophy, was as wide as that of John Stuart Mill, though in an already more specialised age his original contributions were more closely limited to one field. Secondly, he was always intensely interested in the practical application of economic doctrine to the current economic problems of the day. He would, I think, have been in sympathy with the increased demand which arises from the present world depression that economists should contribute what they have to give to the formation of current policy and should equip themselves for this contribution by close contact with the realities of economic activity and organisation.

It is perhaps significant of the present relation of economics to the practical problems of to-day that the first lecturer appointed on this foundation is one who is not, in the strict sense, an economist, having neither the special academic training nor the academic qualifications which most of those in this room possess or will possess before they complete their residence at this University.

The true economist, I suppose, usually acquires his doctrine in the first instance by a deductive process. He draws the conclusions which follow from such basic assumptions as that of "the economic man", and builds his doctrine in the first instance upon conclusions so obtained. With a doctrine so formed, or partly formed, he approaches the study of the actual activities of man, of the economic process as it operates in the complex and intricate variety of real life; and he develops, modifies and applies his original doctrine as seems to be necessary. The original skeleton is clothed afterwards with living tissue. My own process has been the opposite one. For a quarter of a century or so I have been engaged in practical administrative work which in varying degree involved problems for which the guidance of economic doctrine seemed likely to be useful. Under this direct practical stimulus I have tried to learn what I could from economists, have thought about their science, and have sometimes attempted, in the sphere of what one may call applied economics, to test, or develop, or modify, a doctrine by fragments of direct personal experience. I have therefore taken other people's deductive doctrine; but anything I have added for myself has been by an inductive process. Any ideas of my own have, so to speak, been squeezed from experience, not brought to it. Well, there are many avenues to truth, and in economics as elsewhere the inductive method is the complement of the deductive. I was interested to read, a little time ago, a remark of a distinguished Professor of this University about the extent to which, in another sphere, the contributions to applied science had come, not from laboratory research, but from the "artisan thinking about his job". I can claim to be no more in relation to economic problems than the artisan who has thought about his job; and the only kind of contribution that can be expected from such a source is not to the pure science but to the applied science.

Speaking then from the point of view of the practitioner seeking guidance from the scientist, I confess that I have sometimes felt that economists as a whole have not always been as helpful to those beset by the daily problems of policy as they might be. Too often they seem to be divided between economic historians immersed in facts with no guiding thread of principle through the maze, and theoretical economists whose doctrine has no close and visible relation to the actual processes of economic life. I make this general comment here with the less diffidence because I must add in justice that the reproach applies less to Cambridge economists trained in the tradition of Marshall, who studied so profoundly the real activities of men and realised how imperfect a reflection of them was to be found in the abstraction of the "economic man".

It is from this point of view that I have chosen as the title of my present lectures "The Framework of an

Ordered Society", for I believe that the conditions and the methods of supplementing our present economic system with deliberate planning constitute one of the most urgent and difficult problems of our day.

I propose in this first lecture to discuss why planning is now necessary to supplement the working of the competitive price system; to argue that the controls and restrictions of which the world is now full are not examples of planning because they have been improvised by opportunists, and that their replacement by planned control is now essential; and that this task cannot be carried out by Government alone but needs the co-ordinated action of unofficial institutions. In my second lecture I propose to illustrate the kind of institutional self-discipline in the economic system which is, I believe, required as an adjunct to the machine of official Government; and in my third and concluding lecture I propose to discuss the consequent relations between private institutions and the Government, and the possible rôle in this connection of Economic Advisory Councils.

I think it is of the most vital importance that economists should now squarely face the question whether the actual economic life of the world in future is likely to be within a framework substantially like that of the nineteenth century or profoundly different; and if they conclude that the latter is inevitable, that they should work intensively on the question of the modification which that will entail to economic doctrine and especially to its application. I can understand the reluctance of both the economic historian and the theoretical economist to contemplate any really fundamental change in the situation. The former has vividly in his mind the triumphs of the nineteenth century system, which encouraged and harvested the application of scientific invention to industrial technique; so that within a framework merely of law, gold currencies and elementary social safeguards, individual enterprise was free to exploit the riches of the new discoveries, while supply adjusted itself to demand, and each one of an infinitely intricate series of economic processes and activities to every other, without either the painful effort or restrictive discouragements of deliberate planning and control. None at least can withhold an honourable tribute at its passing to a system which sheltered hundreds of millions in a comfort known before only to as many thousands; and which decade by decade absorbed an increasing population and supported it at higher standards of living. The reluctance of the theoretical economist is no less intelligible. To pass from a system in which economic phenomena are determined by the motives of innumerable economic men, whose individual caprices do not exist or cancel out, to one in which they are profoundly affected by the deliberate and fallible reason of a few hundreds, is to pass from a comparatively exact to a mainly empirical science. The theoretical and mathematical science based upon the assumptions that make exact conclusions possible may still remain and cultivate itself with ever-increasing subtlety; but if it fails to adjust itself to facts, it must lose even the semblance of any important relation to the practical life of man. Under a functioning *laissez-faire* system the economist had the best of two good worlds; the satisfaction which intricate and exact intellectual reasoning gives, and the equally pleasing but usually incompatible satisfaction of exercising power. It is a privilege hard to abdicate.

Nevertheless, I believe it is clear that an objective consideration of the actual forces and tendencies now in the world shows conclusively that this situation must be faced. It is indeed possible, as it is certainly to be ardently hoped, that some of the impediments to the free working of automatic adjustments can be removed or reduced, that here and there a field of free action can be cleared. If, however, we consider the factors which, as compared with the last century, are novel in degree and indeed in kind, and which tend to restrict and disturb the normal free adjustments, we shall, I think, realise that the automatic system can never again be relied upon to function as easily and frictionlessly as it did in the past.

Let us take, for instance, the character of the industrial organisation of a considerable part of the largest industries in the most advanced countries. The steel industry in America, for example, is so nearly a monopoly that it can within considerable limits establish the price at which it will sell its products. Such effective competition as exists, in the case of industries organised upon this scale, is a competition with producers of substitute articles (oil instead of coal, etc.) rather than with producers of the same article, and often the most effective force tending to keep prices down is not the competitive price of the article but what the market will stand. The consideration which determines the price that is fixed is based upon whether reduction will tap a large additional demand or increase will kill it. The same is true for a large part of the distributive and commercial organisations, where there are rings or semi-monopolies, or understandings. The consumer loses his "rent" and those with whom the decision rests are able to choose at a time of falling wholesale prices whether they will reduce their own prices correspondingly or lose the chance which reduced prices would give of maintaining or extending their custom. Whenever these conditions apply it is clear that the automatic adjustment of the old system works much less effectively than in the past.

A similar impediment to adaptation is of course created by all the organisations and the forces which tend to make wages rigid. This impediment is of course of special importance at a time when monetary or other causes are creating considerable changes in the general level of prices, but it is of importance at all times. The same is true also of the extending social legislation which has been so rapid a phenomenon of this century, especially in this country.

Not less important than the above factors is economic nationalism, expressing itself in tariff and other commercial policy. This has been steadily growing ever since the war and has now reached a height for which we can find no precedent in recent history. It is true that some of the causes of this movement may be temporary and that some retracing of our steps may be possible. It is difficult, however, to anticipate in any easily foreseeable future that we shall have a system favouring the free movement of trade as much as that of the nineteenth century did, even after the protection initiated by Germany in its later decades. We may reasonably hope for an improvement of the present position in some respects. In particular we may hope that tariffs will become more stable, after the present financial crisis is past. But no prophecy surely could be safer than that, in the world as a whole, tariffs will for many years remain as a principal factor in determining the economic structure of most countries and the volume and character of the trade between them.

When again we turn from the sphere of economics to that of monetary policy and finance, we must surely contemplate not less but more control than was exercised in the years immediately preceding the crisis. The crisis itself indeed has demonstrated the impossibility of a system which combined almost complete freedom in the movement of capital, and in all capital operations, with such severe restrictions upon the movement and distribution of trade.

Wherever we turn, therefore, we have a prospect of extensive control and restriction upon the free development of enterprise and of trade. I have mentioned only some of the more striking examples of permanent and, for the most part, increasing importance. Now all of these, whether they are wise or foolish, whether they are improvised or planned, have one characteristic in common. They interfere with the free working of the automatic system of competitive price adjustment; they make it more rigid and less quickly and readily adaptable.

With this loss of elasticity in the system we are confronted with the other principal phenomenon of our age, the unprecedentedly rapid extension of mechanisation and the improvement in industrial technique, which makes rapid adaptability in the economic system more essential if the most disastrous reactions and dislocations are to be avoided. Every new invention, displacing men, changing the distribution of purchasing power, and consequently the direction of demand, will cause waste and unemployment, unless the economic system is so elastic and responsive as to make the new demand quickly effective, to adjust supply to it, to transfer and absorb the displaced workers. There is indeed much exaggeration and folly associated with the "technocracy" which has recently been so much discussed in America. Many of those who have been dazzled by the staggering results of new technical inventions in particular industries, where a 90 per cent. economy or more has been effected in man-power, have assumed that this represents a process likely to extend in a similar degree over most human activities. This is, of course, a wild exaggeration. Some have fallen into the even more absurd error of thinking that man's increase of power over nature, instead of being as it is a promise of immensely greater prosperity, must inevitably entail permanent and increasing unemployment and impoverishment. Others again have, with equal folly, advocated the adoption, as the basis of currency systems, of a "unit of energy", failing to realise that the physical power used in production bears a changing and diminishing relation to economic values and human activities as a whole; and that it is therefore completely unsuitable either to determine the total amount of currency required at a given period, or to secure adjustment between different human activities, or to afford a measure of relative reward.

It is also true that new technical inventions, in spite of the displacement of labour which they involve, do not constitute the main origin of our present troubles; nor can they be regarded as solely responsible for the continuance of the unemployment which they cause by displacement. It would be more exact to say that when the adaptability and absorptive capacity of the economic system have, for other reasons, been reduced, the rapidity of technical invention is an aggravating factor. "Technological unemployment" is a substantial part of the present unemployment in the world and, in one sense, it can be approximately measured. Three separate estimates, for example, by competent economists have recently put the figure at one million out of the five million out of work in Germany. It would, however, be a mistake to conclude from this that if there were no general depression there would be in Germany a million unemployed through technological displacement. A large proportion of those who have become unemployed through this cause would in other circumstances be absorbed into other work and only remain unemployed now because the depression, itself due mainly to other causes, has temporarily reduced the absorptive capacity of the economic system.

Nevertheless, when we have stripped "technocracy" of all its fallacies and its exaggerations, this at least remains true. The combination of an increase in the rapidity of technical inventions and processes with the increased impediments to automatic adjustment which have been mentioned above must result, in any foreseeable future, in a substantial mass of "technological unemployment", unless we can restore the absorptive capacity of the economic system; and since many of the new impediments to automatic adjustment are likely to be permanent, we can only do this if we supplement it by some form of deliberate planning.

There are indeed, as I have suggested, many special features and causes of the present depression—some of which are unprecedented and will, we may hope, be neither permanent nor recurrent: a mass of indebtedness left after the war; a passionate nationalism expressing itself in economic policy; a monetary disturbance which has resulted from these and in turn has aggravated their consequences. But when all these have been dealt with, or have worked out their own solution, much will remain to differentiate both the system and the problems of our period from those of the last century. I am convinced that the task of the future is not merely that of removing unwise restrictions, though much of this is required, but that of replacing foolish and improvised control by wisely planned control.

I do not think that many will dispute that the great mass of the present restrictions, controls and recent interferences with the working of the automatic system has been improvised, and foolishly improvised. Demonstration is therefore unnecessary, and a few illustrations will suffice to remind us of what we all know.

Let us consider, for example, in broad outline the

character of State action within the sphere of commercial
policy. I do not now propose to discuss the general
merits of Protection and Free Trade. I assume that,
whether we like it or not, some measure of State protection in most countries will be a fundamental feature
in the world's economic system for many years to come.
My present point is that the present tariffs are scarcely
ever the expression of what in any reasonable sense can
be called either national or any kind of policy. It is
rarely possible to discover in the mind of any government a general conception of economic policy for their
country of which their detailed tariffs are the logical
development. Ideas of improving the balance of trade,
or of securing self-sufficiency, or of making the foreigner
pay, float about, but they operate, not to determine the
character and proportions of the actual tariff system, but
merely as arguments and forces to secure the acceptance
of tariffs. The tariffs themselves are selected, and their
height determined, in most cases as the net result of
organised competitive pressures. For some years at
Geneva, during the tariff negotiations there, I tried to
discover what were the real springs of action, what were
really the dominant anxieties and preoccupations in the
minds of Ministers of Commerce and their chief officials
when they were defending existing tariffs or proposing
changes. In nearly every case, when it was possible to
penetrate behind the words to the thoughts of the
persons concerned, it was not a conception, whether
wise or unwise, of general economic national policy, but
a calculation of prospective political forces, that was
determining action. Tariffs as we have them now in the

world have not been planned but improvised, and improvised under organised pressure.

It is the same when we turn from tariffs to other forms of commercial policy. Let us take a few examples from our own country of the selective encouragement by State action of particular kinds of production. The most notable schemes that have been actually put into operation have concerned, in chronological order, rubber, sugar and wheat.

It seems incredible, in retrospect, that any government could have employed official action to enforce a restriction scheme of which the ultimate effect was bound to be merely to profit the Dutch competitor. Had it been possible to secure the inclusion of the Dutch rubber planters, the scheme, whether or not defensible or desirable on other grounds, would at least have been a practicable one. But it should have been obvious, and would have been obvious to any body of competent and disinterested persons who had been given a week to examine the situation, that in their absence nothing but permanent harm could result. What happened was exactly what could have been anticipated. Great profits were made by speculators, and even greater profits by the Dutch planter, who enjoyed the full benefit of the higher prices which the restriction caused, while being himself free not only to continue his full protection but to expand it; and in these circumstances the price ultimately fell again, as it was bound to, but with the difference that the British share of the world market was left on a permanently lower level. When this had happened, and the harm done was irreparable, the scheme was brought to an end. My point is that the explanation of this ill-conceived venture is that a harassed, preoccupied, over-worked and inexpert Government succumbed to the pressure of a concentrated and organised interest, as it is always apt to unless it has at its disposal, and utilises, a machinery and procedure which will provide a safeguard against such follies. Had a committee selected from among such persons as are now associated with the present Economic Advisory Council been called to examine the proposal and report, there can be no doubt that their conclusions would have been strongly adverse. It does not follow, of course, that their advice would have been accepted; the Government might, under the pressure of the interests concerned, have still sinned against the light.

I will now take two examples affecting agriculture in this country—the subsidies given to sugar and wheat. Again, I do not now propose to argue whether, by Government action, and at some public expense to either the taxpayer or the consumer, it is wise to expand agricultural production in this country beyond the point which it would reach under a system of free competition with the outside world. If, however, we assume that this is our policy, surely one thing is clear; that the kind of agricultural production we should especially encourage is that for which the country has the best natural advantages.

Now it is obvious that as regards meat, fruit, poultry and dairy produce, this country has a natural advantage in that all these articles deteriorate in time or lose something of their quality by preservation, so that it is a good thing for the producer to be near his market. In contrast with these, sugar and wheat lose nothing by lapse of time, and cost very little to transport or store. Moreover, owing to the way in which our land is parcelled up, and the tenure under which it is held, we are obviously at a great disadvantage in comparison with other countries from which we might import. Sugar is just as good if it is transported over the world, and is indeed better if it comes from Java or the West Indies where a tropical sun has transmitted sweetness through the cane. Wheat too is obviously produced more advantageously in lands where large spaces facilitate mechanised processes. There is another consideration, too. There is a natural long-term tendency of the world demand for fresh meat, fruit and dairy produce to increase, not only proportionately to the increase of population, but also with a rising standard of living, since they are relatively luxury foods. On the other hand, it had long been obvious that sugar and wheat were likely for years to come to be produced in excess of an almost stationary demand. A policy definitely designed to make us self-sufficient in wheat, in view of the risks of war, would of course be logically defensible, though very expensive and perhaps impracticable. But no such policy was at the basis of our action. If that consideration is excluded it is obvious that a policy of agricultural protection, which had been planned and thought out with care, would have put wheat and sugar at the bottom, not at the top, of its list. It is a good illustration of our present unplanned control that it was these two commodities which were selected for first and special encouragement. The wheat subsidy, at the expense of the consumer, is relatively recent. The sugar subsidy has been in operation long enough for us to see its results. It has proved so extravagant that the public (as taxpayer and consumer) was paying more than £2 for every £1's worth of sugar even before the recent abnormal fall of world prices.

If we turn from commercial policy to monetary policy, the case is perhaps not quite so clear. Here there has obviously been deliberate planning and direction. The planning has, however, been incomplete and to a large extent ineffective. To some extent this is due to the impact of forces of exceptional strength, resulting from war disturbance, both internal and external. Exclude these, however, and we cannot fail to admit in retrospect that, if our own monetary policy was based upon a very definite view of London as a financial centre, and England as a creditor, it was not planned in relation to a balanced view of all the varied interests of the country. It is clear that if there had been an equal consideration of the whole economic situation of the country, with due regard to the new rigidities of the price and wage structure, the pound would not have been so light-heartedly stabilised at 4.86, with the facile assumption, so commonly made by Treasuries trained under a more elastic system, that the economic adjustments of prices would follow automatically.

The instances discussed above of official intervention in schemes affecting production are not isolated or exceptional. On the contrary they are typical of the greater part of the world's commercial policy, which has been built up by successive concessions to interested pressure. It is the most serious, and the most unjust, obstacle to the schemes not only of Socialists but of all those who desire any system in which the public interest is adequately protected by public control, that the present commercial policies of the world constitute a kind of bastard socialism, conceived not in the public interest but pressed upon harassed governments by strong sectional organisations. Nor is this accidental or fortuitous. It results inevitably from the unsuitability of the present procedure and traditions of representative government for the economic tasks of the present period.

It has, I think, become abundantly clear that, for such responsibilities, the machine of government as we know it in countries with free democratic institutions is incompetent. The system, its methods and its traditions, grew up when the bulk of the work of government was political, and its tasks in relation to economic development either secondary or only occasional. There is a complete and fundamental difference between these two categories of tasks, and the kind of government which is suitable for each. Political problems, whether they are internal, turning for example on the extension of the full rights and opportunities of citizenship to hitherto unfranchised or unprivileged classes, or external, turning upon disputes with other countries, may be both difficult and dangerous. But they are relatively simple in their content, discontinuous, disconnected and terminating. A new extension of the franchise is given or denied; a dispute is settled and ended. Each may be a precedent or an occasion for a new problem; but there is not normally any such essential unity or interrelation between them as there is, or should be, between separate and successive measures of economic policy.

For economic problems, however, unless successive acts of government are to lead to continually increasing confusion, deliberate planning, consecutive thinking and careful elaboration of the main policy without the disturbing influence of sectional pressure are essential.

Parliamentary government, as it now operates, makes this impossible. Parliament consists of a heterogeneous mass of persons distinguished from their fellows by the qualities that please electors or party committees, or who have more means and leisure than other men; in their contact with the executive's task of continuous government and elaboration of economic policy they are at once inexpert and sectionally minded, at once ineffective and exacting. In such an environment a Minister cannot plan; he can only improvise. The daily impact of successive visitors, combined with the inconsecutive, troublesome, urgent difficulties of daily administration, pouring in from every sphere of governmental activity and from every quarter of the world, makes consecutive thinking impossible. A modern Minister is *ex officio* an improviser and an opportunist; and he is *ex officio* a weary man—perhaps a weary Titan, but certainly weary. And this is true not only of Ministers, but of the relatively small number of officials who are consulted on major policy. Now, unhappily, the first instinct of every tired man is to reject new or external assistance as likely only to give him new work and worry. On a short view this is always true, and it is always the short view that the tired and overworked man tends to take. The best chance a Government or a Minister has of giving effect to a well-considered and deliberately thought-out policy is that they will have occupied a preceding period of opposition and relative leisure in thinking it out. But this is unlikely and unsatisfactory, for a policy worked out in opposition is likely to be determined too much by reaction from the opposing principles or proposals of rival parties; it suffers from the absence of expert opinion and the sense of responsibility which office gives; and, as events change quickly, it may be out of date. Moreover, the permanent advisers enjoy no such respite or opportunities. They are subject, without intermission, to the successive minor difficulties of daily administration; they see policy from the point of view of these near and narrow problems, and of a single, departmental point of view—and are likely therefore to fail to see the wood for the trees. Departmentalism, a conservative clinging to traditions and precedents unsuited to changed conditions, and an opportunist attitude to such new problems as cannot be ignored, are almost inevitable characteristics of an official system; and unless they are corrected by a wider vision and a more broadly conceived policy brought from outside by Ministers and those consulted by them, the results must be disastrous.

It is in large measure the change in the character of modern tasks of government which explains the discredit, the deterioration, and in many cases the replacement, of free representative institutions. In Russia we have a centralised system which enforces planning at the expense of political, personal and economic liberty alike. In Italy we have a Fascism which, at the expense of political freedom, has retained a measure of controlled economic freedom. In Germany and other countries we see a similar development. Even here, the establishment of the Tariff Advisory Committee, and the reasons by which it was explained, are a tentative step towards the removal from Parliament of powers previously exercised by it. It is becoming clear that either Representative Government must be replaced—at what a terrible price and by what methods I will not stop to enquire—or it must reform itself and its methods. I believe myself that the latter course is practicable. I do not believe that the only alternatives before us are a Communism which destroys both political and economic freedom, or a Fascism which, at the expense of political liberty, leaves a limited freedom for capitalists; or the inefficiency which follows the assumption of new and more complex tasks by a representative government as it now functions. I believe that we can both plan and preserve freedom on three conditions: that Parliaments will delegate some of their functions to the Executive, without abdicating their ultimate responsibility; that the Executive will fit itself for its tasks by welcoming the assistance of those who direct the actual economic activities of the country; and that these in turn will assume the task of collectively controlling and planning their own activities, in association with Government and through an appropriate organisation. The character of this organisation will be the theme of my next lecture.

II

INSTITUTIONAL SELF-DISCIPLINE

In my last lecture I tried to show that an ordered society is essential, that our present controls and restrictions now improvised piecemeal must be replaced by planned control, and that the central organ of Government, with only its professional advisers, was and would remain incapable either of planning on the scale required or even of directing the execution of a planning scheme.

If we are to have a planned and directed economic system, it is from inside that system that we must find those who will, for the most part, plan and control, and they must do this through their own institutions. True, Government can and must play a part, but it can be a part only; and even for that part, of encouragement and general guidance, they will in my view need to utilise the assistance of those who are actively engaged in the economic activities of the country to a much greater extent than at present.

In a word, I believe that our economic system needs to develop an institutional self-discipline, aided but not in detail directed by the Government. I believe this, though difficult, is not impossible, and that it represents the one practicable alternative to increasing inefficiency on the one hand or the establishment of a system incompatible with political and economic freedom on the other.

I propose to suggest very tentatively the lines upon which this institutional self-government might develop. But let me first recall in the most general terms the goal to be attained. Throughout our intricate modern life of varied needs and specialised activities, supply needs to be adjusted to demand and each economic process to the others on which it depends. The automatic adjustments of changing prices under a fully competitive system can no longer be relied upon by themselves, for the reasons I gave in my last lecture, and they need to be supplemented by deliberately planned direction. Each one of our individual activities tends to react destructively upon others, and needs therefore to be kept within a general framework which will prevent such fatal interactions. We must have a system which translates each increase in productive capacity into equivalent purchasing capacity and so enables us to utilise to the full the resources and the skill which are now at our disposal. For this the competitive price system supplemented by a mere system of law, or centrally devised regulations, within the competence of a central government, will no longer suffice. The economic system must develop institutions through which it can to the extent required regulate its own activities; and those who direct it must regard themselves as having, not a single but a double responsibility, first for carrying out their own individual business efficiently, and, second, for constructing, with others engaged in similar activities, a framework of general policy and regulation which will leave the stimulus to individual effort but will prevent the action of the individual, or business concern, from reacting destructively upon others or upon the general public interest.

To some extent this will mean creating new institutions; to some extent transforming those we have. I remember a remark made to me when the world depression was beginning by one who has had an almost unequalled experience of commercial policy in Central Europe. He said in effect: "You in England have a more elaborate system of economic organisations than any other country. You have Chambers of Commerce and Federations of Industry. You have Employers' organisations and Trade Unions which fix wages. You have rings or understandings which, within considerable limits, determine prices. You have social legislation which settles a large part of the overhead costs of every business. We are entering on a period in which great adaptations to changing conditions will be necessary. Your institutions may in this period be a great handicap or they may be a great advantage. If they are used only to resist and postpone changes ultimately necessary, they will be a handicap. But if they could be used to anticipate and accelerate the changes that must eventually come, they might be a great advantage, for they would enable you to make the necessary adaptations that will come more slowly and with great waste from the ruthless operation of blind but compelling economic forces. If, for example, a change in wholesale prices makes possible, and will ultimately compel, a reduction in retail prices, your distributive organisation may postpone it and lose its custom, or it may anticipate what must ultimately come and maintain the volume of business to the general benefit. What you need is to convert your institutions from instruments of resistance to change into instruments of rapid and unwasteful adaptation".

I propose a little later to illustrate the way in which what I have called institutional self-development may develop in the different parts of our system, which concern respectively the control of money, the flow of capital, and industrial organisation. But before entering each of these spheres separately, let me suggest a few principles which will apply throughout.

In the first place we need, I think, to "professionalise" the organisations which at present represent sectional activities. These organisations have usually a double aspect. First, that of defending the special interests of those concerned, either as against directly opposed or competing interests or the public in general; and, secondly, that of developing standards of efficiency and of conduct, of encouraging an internal self-discipline which is in the general public interest. I may call the first the "defensive" and the second the "professional" aspect of these organisations. It is obvious that the proportions in which the two elements are to be found varies very greatly in the case of the different organisations. It is also obvious that at present in most cases the defensive element predominates. Take, for example, such an Employers' Federation as is found in the coal industry. It has become evident in recent years that an organisation was needed which could speak for the industry as a whole and could exercise an effective influence over its constituent units in regard to any general scheme of reform required. The existing organisation, however, was formed primarily for the purpose of defending the interests of employers as such against those of employees as such. The whole traditions of such an organisation were necessarily such as to make it unsuitable for a task that needed to be at once constructive and co-operative. Nor is it only the traditions. It is natural that when for many years an organisation has existed for defensive purposes, the personnel who become associated with it are those who are specially interested in that kind of work. A body whose primary work it has been to contest the claims of labour is likely to be staffed throughout, and directed at the top, by those who think primarily in terms of dealing with every difficulty in terms of reductions of wages rather than improvement of efficiency and reconstruction, and the real constructive intelligences in the industry are likely to be outside and without influence in it.

As an instance of a sectional body of a different type I may cite the General Medical Council, which is more professional in character and is perhaps helped to maintain its professional standards by the existence as a separate organisation of the British Medical Association. The General Medical Council does exist primarily to encourage an improvement in the standards of conduct of the profession, which is in the public interest. It removes the qualifications of doctors who have been guilty of unprofessional conduct in neglecting their patients, etc. Even in the case of a body such as this, however, we sometimes find greater enthusiasm shown in dealing with professional misconduct which injures the pro-

fession—such, for example, as co-operating with an
unqualified practioner—rather than that which injures
the public.

If they are to be the instruments of a planned economic
system, it will be necessary in the above sense to "professionalise" the group organisations that exist, and at
the same time to relate them more directly to those who
really direct action and policy so that they are more
effective in controlling and influencing that policy. It is
also obvious that, whereas existing organisations may,
with modifications and adaptations, cover a certain part
of the ground, they will need to be supplemented in
many cases by new institutions; and these may, in my
view—according to the extent of the general public
interest which is involved—comprise in varying measure
the association of public representatives.

In all these sectional organisations, however, there is
one principle to which I attach great importance and the
observance of which will largely determine the whole
character of a planned system. In my view we need to
conceive of the planned structure of society as always
growing up from below and not enforced from above.
Each controlling authority, if it is to have either the
experience or the influence required, must be constructed
from within itself and not imposed by an external power.
The application of this principle varies of course con-
siderably in the different cases, but it is so important
that I think it may be well to expand a little what I have
to say on the point. I will illustrate it by a problem of
organisation which I found confronting me in connection
with the control of shipping some sixteen years ago. It

had become in 1917 of the utmost importance that the shipping policies of the main Allies in the war—which at that time, through the shortage of shipping, dominated and controlled the whole supply programmes— should be effectively co-ordinated. It was decided to form an Allied Maritime Transport Council. But upon what principle was this Council to be formed? Some proposed that a number of whole-time people should be appointed on a Shipping Board which would be given power to plan and direct the use of all ships at the disposal of the Allies—British, French, American or Italian. It was objected to this proposal, and with reason, that the Shipping or Supply Ministers of the different countries could hardly be expected to delegate to other persons powers which would make their own positions quite subordinate, and would indeed, in view of the extent to which the control of shipping at that time affected every sphere of policy, be tantamount to asking the Governments themselves to abdicate, as regards a large measure of their responsibility, in favour of a new authority external to themselves. Such an authority was unlikely to be given and, if given, would certainly be withdrawn. A counter-proposal was therefore made, that the Shipping Board should not be executive but advisory, that it should make its plans and then advise each Government to accept and carry out the part which fell within its own province. It was, however, objected with equal reason that, if the first proposal involved the delegation of too much power, the second involved too little; a mere advisory board would be completely impotent to secure the action necessary.

And then came the discovery. A Shipping Council was formed, and constituted into both a planning and executing authority, by the appointment of the actual Shipping and Supply Ministers of the different countries, who continued to exercise their national functions, but became for a time and for a definite purpose, as members of an international organ, not National but Allied Ministers. This principle of organisation avoided the dilemma of choosing between either an impossibly powerful or a hopelessly weak planning authority. For the plan made by a body so composed was necessarily adjusted to the policies and interests of the different governments as well as their common interest, and the action agreed to by each member in his international capacity was afterwards executed in his national capacity as Minister of his own country. This vital principle, which has since been expressed in the Council of the League of Nations, is one which needs, I suggest, to be at the basis of the whole structure of any planned society. So only shall we get realism in our plans, competent and effective execution of them, and self-government in the most real sense throughout the economic structure.

The next main question that arises is how far planning must go both extensively and intensively; what can be left outside its scope, and how far control must penetrate down to the detail of every activity. Upon the answer to these questions, of course, depends what measure of real economic freedom planning leaves with us and, indeed, what measure of political freedom either. We shall see some answer to these questions as we come to the different spheres of activity. In the meantime it is sufficient to suggest that the ideal should be, first, to see, when arranging any particular measure of control, that the range of its reactions and consequences are foreseen and dealt with by any necessary complementary planning, but, secondly, that—subject to this—the maximum scope for free adjustments and free enterprise should be left. No more control should ever be imposed than is required to prevent the free activities of individuals from causing more damage in their impact upon each other than they add directly to the common good.

With these principles in mind, what, in each main sphere, would be the main institutions and their functions?

At the centre, of course, is the authority controlling the currency. Here we have, nationally, in the Bank of England an institution which in some measure has the characteristics of the institutions which I wish to see more generally extended. The Bank is legally a private institution under charter. But in fact it fulfils vital public functions and has developed traditions corresponding to those functions. Its most severe critics do not allege that its decisions, as to Bank rate, etc., are determined by considerations as to whether a high or low rate would be more beneficial to the shareholders' dividends; and it is evident that if its present traditions were abandoned, and the Bank actuated in its policy primarily by profit-making motives, its constitution would have to be changed or its privilege withdrawn. What is alleged, however, is that the Bank is influenced in its policy, not by its own shareholders' interests, but by those of the environment in which it mainly lives and works, that of the financial interests of the City of London as distinct from industry and commerce or the economic life of the country as a whole. What, if any, changes then are needed? Well, it is clear that the ultimate decisions as to the main basis of the national currency must rest, as they do, with the Government and Parliament, who must decide, for example, whether the currency should be on gold, and if so at what parity it should be fixed. But surely the authority of those who represent the general public interest should extend further. The Bank surely ought not to decide itself, on its own authority and with its present constitution, whether policy should, for example, during a given period, be directed towards securing an upward or a downward movement of prices. The Bank is admirably fitted to be an executant of general policy but not to determine it. Main policy should, I suggest, be laid down by the Government, which in turn should itself be advised by persons reflecting the views of those engaged in all the main activities of the country. The machinery through which this advice might be given is suggested in what follows.

Currency questions, more than any other, lead inevitably to a consideration of international co-operation. It will suffice at this point to remark that the informal co-operation between the Governors of the principal Central Banks, which has been developing since the war, has now been supplemented by the creation of an International Bank—the Bank for International Settlements. This institution—with a suitable extension of its powers—could serve as the instrument of whatever world monetary policy is decided upon. Its directing authority is constituted of those who control the national Central Banks—and it is therefore their collective instrument of action. It is thus founded upon the fundamental principle just suggested, that the directing authority should not be external and imposed but a collective expression of the constituent elements whose co-operation is required. The International Bank, so composed and so controlled, could be made the main world instrument for guiding both monetary and financial policy. It could, for example, be used at present first to help world prices up and then to maintain the general level of prices reasonably stable.

Next we come to the system which directs the flow of capital. Here I should like to see several types of new institutions. First I think we need the kind of National Investment Board which Mr Maynard Keynes has been advocating. This Board in my view should include, but not consist mainly of, Government officials. It should have powers, which should be exercised sparingly, to forbid public issues temporarily (or in extreme cases permanently) for specified purposes. We have at present a practical embargo imposed when and as the Treasury thinks fit. The exercise of such powers—not less effective for being based upon no legal authority—by a Department which does not state its reasons and is likely to be actuated by a single point of view in what may be a very complex situation is obviously not justifiable except as a temporary and emergency measure, and in the absence of any regular institution. In addition to its rarely exercised veto, the National Investment

Board would in my view fulfil a more important function in improving the whole mechanism through which capital is obtained from the investor for new issues, and in particular issues for new concerns. I need not dilate on the scandals connected with company promotion, perhaps the least creditable part of the whole of our system. My main point is that, with provision for prohibiting certain issues and with an improved mechanism for the guidance of the new investor, the main flow of capital could be left to find its way freely, guided by the ordinary economic motives.

As regards permitted foreign lending, something rather different is, I think, required. The amount allowed to be issued might be limited by the Investment Board, but the direction of the permitted foreign investment must depend on the individual investor and on the issuing houses to which he looks for advice. A substantial part of the cause of the financial collapse of 1931 is to be found in the reckless and ill-directed lending (especially to Governments and public authorities) of the years 1924–1928. Foreign issuing houses cannot be absolved of a serious responsibility. They could now, without great difficulty, prevent the danger of similar abuses in the future. Half-a-dozen houses in New York and even a smaller number in London and Paris have the matter in their hands. They could collaborate in drawing up a code setting out the conditions and safeguards desirable for different classes of foreign loans—especially those to public authorities. And if they then used their collective influence to discourage issues that did not comply with these conditions, they could make it impossible for any would-be "blacklegging" house to tempt the investor after his recent experiences. So much for negative action. Positively I believe the reluctant investor could be both encouraged and safeguarded by the creation of a few specialised institutions such as the one recently recommended by the League of Nations for agricultural mortgage loans in distant countries.

In some cases the co-operation of the Stock Exchanges and the Banks is needed to deal with an abuse. The speculative boom in America and the following crash were the opening chapters of the great depression. The crash was proportionate to the speculative boom which preceded it; and the extent of this in turn was due to the facilities which the small and ignorant investor has to speculate on margins and on borrowed money. There ought surely to be some machinery to restrict these facilities at a time when a dangerous speculative boom is in progress.

It will probably be conceded that, if a reasonable amount of constructive intelligence and collective determination is available, the worst defects in the world's currency and credit system could be remedied. This alone, however, is obviously not enough, and we enter a much more difficult sphere when we come to industrial production. In the case of a number of the most important industries—iron and steel, motor-cars, etc.— it is clear that the efficacy of the self-adjusting system has been largely destroyed. The existence of very large concerns, with many of the powers of monopolies but no machinery for effectively planning production in relation to demand throughout the whole of the markets they serve, is likely to be the source of frequent and perhaps increasing crisis of over-production, and more and more intense slumps after booms. Such organisations have financial resources, and credit with the public enabling them to raise additional resources, which makes them independent of the monetary system and makes it possible for them to defeat, if they wish to, the attempts of a central monetary authority to deflate a boom which is becoming dangerous. Their resources make it possible for them to continue full production for a time when, under a system based upon smaller units, falling prices would have rapidly adjusted supply to a reduced demand. Then, when it has become clear that it will not be possible to sell at existing prices, they still have enough control of the market to give them a choice between reducing prices or losing custom; and just when the general situation makes the former course most desirable they often choose the latter.

All this is true. But two important considerations which tend to make the problem soluble need equally to be borne in mind. The first is that where a large-scale organisation of this kind has developed it can itself, without insuperable difficulty, be made the instrument of the new direction that is required. Corporations which are powerful enough to resist the adjustments forced upon weaker concerns under the automatic, competitive system, may, with no impossible development of collaboration, be also powerful enough to secure those adaptations by deliberate decision, and without either the delay or the loss that the competitive process involves. They also constitute ready-made units for a wider organisation which can guide policy throughout the whole world sphere of the particular industry. The second consideration, no less important, is that a system of this kind need not comprehend all industries. If, in addition to a reform of the monetary and financial system, the dangers to equilibrium arising from the competitive over-expansion of the great basic industries which are organised in large units can be arrested, the general system would be sufficiently stabilised to enable the ordinary free automatic adjustments to work as at present, without intolerable waste or dislocation, throughout the large field of industrial enterprise which remains organised in smaller units. Not even in the case of the few large-scale industries is more than a partial replacement of the competitive system necessary. Each unit would normally be conscious of the effect of external competition and would be guided in its policy by the same considerations as at present. But, by being linked up with such a system as I am now proposing, it would be assisted in the determination of its own policy; and the different units in the same industry would be able to deal collectively with the special needs that arise, for example, at the crucial points of a trade-cycle.

I should exceed both the scope of my theme, and the limits of my time, if I attempted to forecast the type of organisation appropriate to different types of industry. It is evident, however, that developments which have already taken place in many industries foreshadow an instrument of direction and control through which many of the present dislocations of production and markets could be prevented. But the organisation will vary in different industries and countries and will change with time and changing needs. Nor need I dilate upon the special problems of agriculture, where the multiplication of small units in production will involve a somewhat different division of functions between Government and producers as regards any regulative control that may be required. My object is only to suggest some of the main principles upon which economic self-government may develop.

Perhaps the main character of the kind of structure which I am suggesting will already have begun to emerge.

A monetary system directed as in the past, but with international co-operation, through a machinery both national and international; the relatively automatic operation of accidental gold supplies being replaced, as it can be, by deliberate policy. An investment system, both national and international, directly controlled as to a small part by the prohibition of specified issues, but otherwise free as in the past, except for the improvement of the machinery for giving advice and information. In industry, the co-operation of the leaders of the greatest concerns in the task of anticipating and mitigating the movements of the trade-cycle, but by methods which still leave them subject in the main and at normal times to the ordinary operation of competitive forces; and the continued free operation of the competitive price system over the rest of industry, subject only to the customary restraints of law and social regulation. In agriculture such planning and control as may prove necessary, guided more directly by a Government suitably advised.

Throughout all these spheres appropriate organs of control and guidance would be developed by the appointment of committees and councils, not imposed from above but appointed from within and composed of those engaged in separate individual enterprises; so that each leader in a country's economic life would have a double rôle and function, that of managing his own concern and that of assisting in constituting the framework within which it operates. The whole of these sectional planning and guiding authorities would be linked together by the formation of wider councils, drawing their membership by selection from the smaller councils, and culminating nationally in National Economic Councils, and internationally in a World Economic Council; these councils being suitably related to the Governments, so that the whole system would be an adjunct to—or rather an integral part of—the machine of Government.

This system would in principle grow up from below, not be imposed as an external and superior set of ruling institutions from above. Logically, therefore, the constitution of each smaller unit should precede the creation of a large one. In fact, however, the general plan must largely be not only made but initiated centrally. And pending the growth and proved competence of the smaller units, the larger units must doubtless be appointed on a selective and not a representative basis. But the constant effort should be to develop the whole pyramidal system in such a way that each stage up to the apex should be based upon the stage immediately below.

In this way we may hope to get a system which supplements the now defective automatic system of competitive price adjustment by the minimum of deliberate regulation and control. It leaves economic freedom in a double sense; first that, subject to a more effective and complete framework of law and regulation, the vast bulk of the adjustments of economic process are still left to the operation of competitive price, and enterprise is left free, with the stimulus of profits; and second, that such measure of additional regulation as is required is both devised and applied through a system of economic self-government. The economic system would thus supply the institutional self-discipline required to deal with its own defects. And lastly, under such a system the central responsibility of the political organs of government would be so lightened and shared that, though political reform would still be necessary, there would be no need of a change of system of so fundamental a character as to involve the sacrifice of political freedom.

We arrive, therefore, at a planned society compatible with both economic and political freedom.

This system obviously needs, however, to be linked up to the organs of political government; and the relations which are involved, I suggest, through a form of improved and developed National Economic Council, will be discussed in my next and concluding lecture.

III

THE RÔLE OF GOVERNMENTS AND
ECONOMIC ADVISORY COUNCILS

In my last lecture I tried to present a sketch of a
self-governing and self-regulating economic structure,
based upon specialised institutions and group organisations. I believe that this is the kind of structure of
society which is likely to develop ultimately from the
stress and strain of this period of transition and trans-
formation; and that it is the system which has the best
chance of combining the planned regulation and control
which has now become necessary with the essentials of
both economic and political freedom. The merit of such
a system is that it would at once relieve government of
an intolerable burden, and free economic enterprise and
development of the dead hand of the kind of control
which, exercised by government as we know it, cramps,
restricts and destroys both variety and elasticity.

Nevertheless, no institutional self-discipline in the
economic system can develop so perfectly and so completely as to make it unnecessary for government itself
to assume and continue vast responsibilities in regard to
the economic life of the country.

In the first place, such a system cannot be expected to
grow spontaneously throughout every sphere of activity
in which it is required. A lead must be given; general
guidance and direction must be forthcoming; if the

Government need not plan in detail, it must "plan planning".

In the second place, there will sometimes be a need for powers which can be given only by Parliament, on the advice of the Government, to deal with resistant minorities.

In the third place, there will be a continuing task of seeing that the institutions which develop in different spheres are co-ordinated with each other.

In the fourth place, the development at the best will be unequal; it will need stimulating, reinforcing, and supplementing where it is weakest.

In the fifth place, there will always be the danger that the "defensive" aspect of a sectional institution will outbalance its "professional" aspect; that it will use the powers which organisation, and often some degree of monopoly, give to exploit rather than serve the public interest. Government itself, which alone derives its authority from the public as a whole, must remain the ultimate guardian of the public interest. It may delegate its responsibility, but it cannot abdicate. It must determine the conditions upon which sectional institutions can grow and work so as to be in the public interest; it must watch their actual working; and any delegation of responsibility must continue only on condition that, and so long as, the trust is honoured and the public interest served.

In the sixth place, there are many forms of economic activity, and there will be more, where not only is the public interest vitally involved but where monopoly is desirable. In such cases some form of public ownership and control will probably be required. This does not of course mean direct management by a Government Department like the Post Office. All sorts of mixed systems are practicable, of which the Central Electricity Board, the Port of London Authority, and the B.B.C. are examples in this country and of which Germany provides more numerous and more varied instances. These again will involve considerable work and responsibility for the Central Government, in determining the conditions appropriate to each case, in making appointments, in watching the due observance of both the letter and the spirit of the charters given, and in considering whether later experience or changing conditions necessitate a modification in the original charters.

Lastly, Government will of course have duties with which we are familiar in regard to the public finances, commercial policy and so on.

Is it not clear that for such tasks the machinery of government must be strengthened and its methods improved? The solution should, I believe, be of two kinds. There should be a change in the relations of Parliament to the Executive; and the Executive itself should arrange to be continuously advised, through an appropriate organisation, by those in direct touch with the country's economic activities.

The first of these reforms lies a little outside my theme, and I cannot now discuss in detail the form which it should take. It is so important a supplement, however, to any general scheme of economic government that a few comments are necessary.

If Ministers in office usually become increasingly

incapable of consecutive thinking, the explanation is to be found only partly in the greater range and complexity of the problems now presented to them. It is equally due to the Parliamentary environment in which they work. Throughout the greater part of the year they are exposed to daily questioning, and frequent debates, on the details of their administrative action; their bills are subject not only to criticism in main principle but amendment in every detail; the drain on time and energy involved is doubled by the personal representations and pressures which are added to these public proceedings. This system worked well enough when the issues were mainly political and relatively simple. It does not work now. It is indeed visibly breaking down throughout a great part of the world. If Parliaments are to retain their essential powers, and to discharge their first responsibility to the public, on which free government depends, it looks as if they must voluntarily surrender the powers and rights which are less essential and which they are least competent to exercise. Suppose for example that Parliaments met for only two or three months of the year. In that time they could approve in main principle the legislation to be enacted for the ensuing year, leaving its detail to be worked out and applied by Order in Council; they could review the action of the Executive during the preceding year and either, by approving it, give it a future lease of life, or, by censuring, secure a change and the appointment of a new Cabinet. Ministers would then have three-quarters of the year to work out, in conjunction with those best qualified to advise them, the general policy for which they had received a mandate. With this reform each part of the body politic would discharge the function for which it is best qualified. Let me take an example. The electorate as a whole is qualified, and entitled, to say what shall be the main character of its economic structure; whether, for example, it desires to be predominantly industrial and as an aid to that ambition to buy its food in the cheapest world markets; or whether, alternatively, it desires a more balanced system under which, at a necessary cost to its industrial expansion and perhaps to its average standard of living, its agricultural production could be expanded. The electorate having through their choice between candidates expressed their views on this major issue of policy and constituted a Parliament, Parliament itself is qualified to lay down the main principles by which the desired end shall be sought; whether for example it shall be through quotas, tariffs, marketing schemes, controlled prices, controlled production, etc. The Government then is best qualified, if it utilises not only its permanent advisers but those who have direct knowledge of agriculture, to elaborate the scheme in detail. And lastly the scheme would be best applied through an organisation created by agriculturists themselves, supervised and guided but not directed in detail by the organs of Government. I take this example with no intention of expressing any opinion on this particular issue of policy but only of illustrating what would seem to be the best division of function in carrying it through. The electorate, while competent to express its view as to main objective, cannot effectively deal with methods even in main principle. Parliament is competent to consider and lay down principles but is likely to cause administrative confusion if it actually drafts the details of a bill. Government can work out these details if it is left reasonably free to do so, and utilises the proper advice; and the public has its safeguards in the limiting principles laid down by Parliament and the latter's power to change the Cabinet. And lastly the industry itself can better, with guidance, apply its own scheme of control through its own organisation, than work under detailed orders from a central authority.

The first reform needed then is a delegation of power from Parliament to the Executive; the second is the utilisation by the latter of specialised external advice, to supplement the help of its own permanent advisers.

In order that this external advice may be effective, available, and utilised, an appropriate organisation will be required. This might take the form of a kind of National Economic Council. It would be a mistake, however, to conceive of such a Council as a kind of Economic Parliament with a large and relatively unchanging personnel consulted as a whole on each economic problem that arises. If it is to be effective, it must include not only a Council capable of occasionally discussing general questions of policy but a flexible machinery through which a few of the best qualified specialists can be made quickly available for the particular problem of the moment. It will be an organisation, pivoting on a small central staff, and normally working through small temporary committees. It should be increasingly linked up with the economic institutions already discussed, but not so closely that the

expert character of the various committees is subordin-
ated to the object of making them "representative", or
that the flexibility of the advisory methods is impaired.

I think that the movement for the establishment of
Economic Advisory Councils which has been taking place
through the world during the last decade is extremely
remarkable and significant. We have some such body,
through which representative persons with experience
of the main economic activities of the country are brought
into association with the Government, in operation in
France, Germany, Italy, Poland, Belgium, Czecho-
slovakia, Spain and Greece, and I have myself been invited to make plans on the spot for similar organisations
in China and India; while successive special enquiries,
serving in part the same purpose, have been conducted
in the U.S.A. and Australia.

Now the important thing about this movement is, not
that these Councils have proved their utility. They have
not. Their functions and constitutions differ greatly, and
the right form of body has probably not yet been dis-
covered—certainly it has not proved itself. But the
extent of the movement, which has developed spontaneously in so many countries, demonstrates clearly a
widely felt need to supplement the existing machine of
government. The more onerous and intricate economic
duties falling upon, or thrust upon, Governments; the
manifest inadequacy both of Governments to discharge
these duties and of the Parliamentary machine—over-
worked, political in outlook and tradition, and un-
specialised—to ensure adequate contact between official
policy and unofficial opinion, are throughout the world

resulting in experiments which vary in form but are obviously designed to meet similar, and universal, needs.

In creating these new Councils the world has been feeling, or fumbling, its way towards a remedy for the obvious defects of the previous system of government. Unhappily the task of discovering the right kind of organisation has been difficult and its establishment slow. The fact is that mere Advisory Councils of men of varied experience but varying ability constitute a very small contribution to the real problem. They can be no sub-stitute for an efficient system extending throughout the main activities of the country; and in any case their own methods of work and machinery need to be devised and applied with great skill upon principles which are in many respects novel. All this means long and difficult constructive work inspired by real creative intelligence. And in the meantime events have been marching fast, straining the whole social system and often transforming the political system into a form incompatible with freedom. This step, however, has not yet been every-where taken, and when it has been taken it may be retraced. It is worth while therefore to examine the results of these new experiments in government, and to consider the conclusions which they suggest. In general Economic Advisory Councils have so far been unsuccessful. But I believe that they embody an idea which, if developed along the right lines, may prove a real contribution to the fundamental problem of govern-ment of our age. Let us look, then, at some of the experiments actually made.

The new institutions embody, in very varying proportions, two different principles and purposes; that of securing *expert* advice and that of securing *representative* advice.

In Germany, for example, the latter principle is dominant. The Reichswirtschaftsrat consisted of no less than 300 persons, most of whom were appointed by organisations representing the main branches of economic activity. The object was to secure a collective expression of the opinions and wishes of these national organisations, and, as a counterpart, to secure a better understanding by them of the policy adopted by the Government. The result was a cumbrous and unworkable institution; and the practical work was carried on by a small central committee.

In France the representative principle also is the main basis; but the actual work has so far been predominantly in the nature rather of enquiries into facts than the formulation of policy, though recommendations are sometimes made. The other European institutions tend to have somewhat the same character as the French or to be something between that and the German system. The Italian organisation is in some respects particularly interesting, as the ideal of the "corporative system" is a form of institutional self-discipline. It must, however, be remembered that, so far, the corporative system is an unrealised ideal, as only the sectional "syndicates", whose union is to form the "corporation", have been actually formed, and the Central Government fulfils the functions ultimately allotted to the corporation.

In this country the Economic Advisory Council is based on a different principle and is primarily designed for a different purpose, namely not that of representing different classes of opinion but that of giving *expert* advice. It is designed throughout to give private expert advice to the Government, as the latter may desire. It not only meets in private but so far it has, with rare exceptions, issued no public reports, recommendations or statements. It is small in numbers and, though it includes the main categories of expert qualifications and experience, it is not "representative" in the sense that the members are expected to express the opinions of any organisations with which they are connected. Its Chairman is the Prime Minister of the time, and several other Ministers are *ex officio* members. It studies only such questions as it is asked to by the Government, or one of the Ministerial members on its behalf. It furnishes its reports in private and these are circulated to the Ministers and Departments concerned; and it normally works through a flexible and convenient system of small committees, formed partly of members of the Council (one of whom presides) and other persons added *ad hoc*.

This bare description gives no true conception of the real character of the organisation, and of either its value or its weakness. These can only be judged by considering how it works. The Council itself hardly ever meets in full session, and seems to have given up doing so. The rare meetings of the full Council are the only ones that are publicly announced, and even then the bare fact of the meeting, or perhaps the general subject discussed, is all that is stated. The general public opinion therefore is probably that it is a defunct institution which does no work and exercises no influence. The public is mistaken in thinking that no work is done; as to whether it is mistaken in thinking that it has no influence is a question more difficult to answer. The fact is that the real work of the Committee is done through small committees, appointed on the initiative of a Minister, usually the Prime Minister, and with the aid of a small but extremely efficient secretariat. These committees, which comprise some of the busiest and best qualified men both in finance and industry, work hard and well; their reports are often of great interest and first-rate quality. Their value, however, depends less on their intrinsic merits than on the use to which they are put. They might serve to inform the public if they were not kept secret; they may influence the policy of the Government to the extent—difficult to judge—to which they are seriously considered. I personally regard it as very regrettable that the reports, or most of them, are not at once published. There is very rarely anything in them of which the publication would be in any way against the public interest—and that little could easily be omitted— unless it is regarded as against the public interest that the public should be aware of the collective opinions of a number of experts, chosen by the Government itself, on certain subjects of current economic problems to which the Government of the day may at the time be paying little attention. Of course the reports would not usually be read by the general public, but they would be read by all those who are writing on current problems, and the whole public discussion of such problems would to the general advantage be improved. As it is, the reports have, and can only have, a value proportionate to the attention given to them by the Minister and Departments concerned. And at this point we confront the psychology of Ministers and officials harassed by pressure and immediate difficulties. The inclination of tired men is to disregard outside advice which is unaccompanied by pressure; and it is a natural instinct of permanent advisers to react against the advice of the external amateur. The consequence is that work, requiring the attendance at meetings over successive weeks, of very busy men may be hastily read or not read at all by the Ministers who alone have the power to give effect to what is recommended; or a collective recommendation may be quietly killed by a brief departmental minute whose nature may not be disclosed to the Committee.

This is of course part of a larger question, which affects a much wider field of work than that of the Economic Advisory Council—namely the whole attitude of Government, of Parliament and the Departments, to the advice which they seek from persons outside the Governmental machine. Commissions, Committees and Conferences are appointed in rapid succession. They occupy the time of experienced and busy men of goodwill for months. An examination in retrospect of the extent to which their work has resulted in action is an extremely discouraging one. This is due to several causes. Sometimes it may be suspected that the real object of a Government is to obtain, not advice, but an excuse for delay; sometimes even to occupy and muzzle persons who would have pressed opinions upon them frequently and by inconvenient methods. Often the terms of reference are inadequately considered; often the personnel hastily or carelessly chosen. The result is extremely serious if the general view presented in these lectures is a true one—if over all the main spheres of the country's economic life it is important that persons engaged in private enterprise should take a large part in determining the conditions and policy which form the framework for their activities, and that those who direct the country's economic life should be associated with government, and form an adjunct to its mechanism. For there is only one, but that a vital, condition on which this association, together with the advice of those outside the central machine, can be secured as a help in the formation of policy—and that is that the persons invited to do this work should have a reasonable expectation that their time will not be wasted. To begin with, they all have at least the illusion that their work will be utilised. One day, however, I fear, an investigator— perhaps a research student of this University—will make a comprehensive study of the fate of the work of Commissions and Committees appointed by Governments; the record will be a disillusioning one, and when its meaning has been realised it may become increasingly difficult to secure the services of the most experienced— and consequently the busiest—men in private enterprise.

I believe that this would be a great disaster, because, for the reasons I have given, I believe that the directing ability and experience in all the main economic activities of the country must take its part in the task of "governance", in constituting and adapting the framework of law, regulation and policy within which individual activities must develop, and for this purpose

7-2

must be suitably associated with the central organs of government.

It is therefore to be hoped that the customary attitude of Government, Parliament and the Departments to advice from those outside their own members will in time be changed. I think that the mechanism and methods of seeking and utilising such advice should be revised in such a way as to secure that it is more regularly and extensively obtained; that it is utilised to the utmost possible effect; and that it is closely related to, and representative of, the directing institutions by which throughout the economic structure the economic life of the country is guided and controlled.

To illustrate what I mean I will mention the lines upon which I suggest the functions of the Economic Advisory Council might usefully develop.

First I think it should, in its methods of working, gradually approximate more nearly to the idea of a General Economic Staff, out of which—as presented by Sir William Beveridge—it originated. This would mean *inter alia* that it would normally have referred to it questions covering the more important aspects of current economic policy. These would not necessarily include, at least to begin with, the most controversial and fundamental questions, on which the Government might take a prior decision. But supposing, at a given moment, the Government decided that tariffs or other restrictions were desirable to relieve a strain on the currency. The Council, through an appropriate committee, might then advise as to the most appropriate principles and methods to apply for that purpose. Or the Government might decide to give protection to industry, on the ordinary protectionist grounds. The Council might then advise as to the principles on which (assuming the main policy) the tariff would most advantageously be constituted. Both protectionists and free-traders, for example, might agree that either the most good (or the least harm, as they would respectively put it) would result from extending the range of an activity for which a country is especially suited rather than by bringing into existence one for which it is quite unsuited. The Tariff Advisory Committee is not really suited for the work of developing such main principles of policy. It has certain advantages, in relieving the Government from the constant pressure of sectional interests; it has the detachment, and something of the impartiality, of a judicial organ. But a judicial authority needs a law to apply and interpret. You cannot refer political problems turning upon a change in existing law to a Hague Court; and the Tariff Advisory Committee has no law, or doctrine, or worked-out general policy to apply. Or supposing, again, that the Government decides to encourage British agriculture, it would be a great advantage if a considered study were available as to the direction in which it could most advantageously direct its efforts—and its necessarily limited resources. It is no accident that the first two forms of production encouraged, at great expense, have been sugar and wheat, for which Great Britain has least advantages.

Secondly, I think that the reports of the Council and its Committees should normally be published, only such reports or passages being withheld as either their authors, or the Government by deliberate decision, decide to be unsuitable for publication.

Thirdly, I think the present system of committees (including both members and non-members of the Council) should be continued and extended; that there should be no permanent committees, and that every committee should be terminated as soon as its activity has ended. But the Council might meet in full session at least once a year; review the work of all the committees during the preceding year; and suggest—though not determine—special subjects or special committees, the decision resting with the Government.

Lastly, I think the future development of the Council should depend upon its proved ability and utility; upon the reputation it has earned; and, in time, upon the extent to which it can represent the final link between the unofficial economic institutions and the Government. In regard to this central institution, as to all secondary or more specialised ones, I think that Government and Parliament, the ultimate guardians of the public interest, should delegate conditionally and gradually but without abdication. In time an enlarged Council, linked up with subsidiary group organisations, might largely serve the purposes of an "economic parliament"—but a subordinate Parliament. No such functions, however, should be allowed to interfere with the flexible and convenient system of small, *ad hoc*, advisory committees utilising the machinery of the Council.

As regards Commissions, etc., I think the whole tradition needs to be similarly changed. The Government might well regard itself, and be regarded, as making its main commitment—subject to an ultimate power of rejection, rarely to be exercised, when a Commission is appointed and its task assigned. The terms of reference ought to be so drafted, and the personnel so chosen, that *on the defined issue* the collective authority of the Commission should be regarded as practically decisive. It ought to be regarded as a reproach—except in the event of decisive and unforeseeable later events—that a Government should have appointed a Commission, consisting of persons chosen by itself, and entrusted with a task defined by itself—and should then come to the conclusion that either itself, or some other persons, were better qualified to decide on the same question.

It is of course obvious that no external rules could secure the result desired. If such rules as the above, for example, were forced on a reluctant administration, which was in fact jealous of outside advice, the obvious administrative device would be to add deliberately to each Commission one or two persons who could be relied upon to insist upon departmental views and, if necessary, to prevent unanimity. Nothing of the kind of development I am picturing is possible unless the political organs of Government definitely desire, and take all possible means to secure, external assistance.

In discussing so vast a question in the space of a few hours, I have necessarily had to be content with the barest and baldest outline. And even the outline has often been rather slightly sketched than drawn firmly. I have tried, not so much to give an ordered and logical description of a mechanism of planning, as to comment upon some of the issues that arise in such a way as to suggest lines of thought and study to my listeners. I am not attempting to make any novel contribution either to economic thought or practical policy. The conception of a planned society has captured the imagination of the public in many different parts of the world and inspired a great deal of study and investigation, both individual and collective. But individual conceptions of the kind of planned society differ widely. These rather inconsecutive comments will perhaps have indicated the general character of my own. I believe we can find a real alternative to a Communism which destroys both political and personal liberty, or a Fascism which at least seriously curtails the first; to a restrictive state socialism directing everything from the centre and to an unregulated *laissez-faire*, which we cannot recover if we would, and any attempt at which will cause the continuance or the recurrence of our present economic troubles. To find this middle, or new, way is the distinctive task of our age. It will not be found by a mere compromise, by taking a middle line, between extremes. The compromise, if such we call it, must be creative and selective, uniting the best that other systems have to offer and avoiding their worst dangers and defects. Such a selective system will, I believe, be based upon the conception of self-government in industry, and in every other sphere of economic activity, but a conditional self-government, encouraged and guided by the constitutional and representative government of the state, dependent for its extent and its development upon being so exercised as to be consistent with the public interest, of which those who draw their authority from the electorate must remain the ultimate arbiters.

I am convinced that it is only by the utilisation of all the constructive and directing skill and experience of the country in the task of controlling and directing specialised activities that we can face the problems of our period and secure a planned society which will on the one hand prevent the suicidal impact of particular activities upon each other, and on the other hand will preserve the essentials of both economic and political freedom. Man has accomplished half his task; he has wrested enough of Nature's secrets from her to give the material basis of a high civilisation to every country in the world; to provide not only the necessities but the comforts of life to the whole of the world's teeming population. The other—and the more difficult—half remains; that of controlling his own human relationships, and directing his own activities so that they are not mutually destructive. The distinctive task of our age is not to extend scientific achievement but to improve the regulative mechanism of government in its widest sense. Among the ideas that will help in this task I believe that of economic self-government to be one of the most promising.

Printed in the United States
By Bookmasters